T0134788

A Letter to Africa About Africa

By Kasongo Munza

Copyright © 2020 Kasongo Munza.

All rights reserved. No part of this book may be used or reproduced by any means, graphic, electronic, or mechanical, including photocopying, recording, taping or by any information storage retrieval system without the written permission of the author except in the case of brief quotations embodied in critical articles and reviews.

To use material in this book, please contact:
Name: Joel K Munza
Email: jojomunza@gmail.com
Phone: 386-795-6127

WestBow Press books may be ordered through booksellers or by contacting:

WestBow Press
A Division of Thomas Nelson & Zondervan
1663 Liberty Drive
Bloomington, IN 47403
www.westbowpress.com
1 (866) 928-1240

Because of the dynamic nature of the Internet, any web addresses or links contained in this book may have changed since publication and may no longer be valid. The views expressed in this work are solely those of the author and do not necessarily reflect the views of the publisher, and the publisher hereby disclaims any responsibility for them.

Any people depicted in stock imagery provided by Getty Images are models, and such images are being used for illustrative purposes only. Certain stock imagery © Getty Images.

Foreword copyright © 2005 Dr. David N. Persons

Scripture quotations taken from The Holy Bible, New International Version® NIV® Copyright © 1973, 1978, 1984, 2011, by Biblica, Inc. TM. Used by permission. All rights reserved worldwide.

Scripture taken from the New King James Version® Copyright © 1982 by Thomas Nelson. Used by permission. All rights reserved.

Scripture taken from the King James Version of the Bible.

ISBN: 978-1-9736-8959-1 (sc)
ISBN: 978-1-9736-8960-7 (e)

Library of Congress Control Number: 2020907062

Print information available on the last page.

WestBow Press rev. date: 04/27/2020

WESTBOW
PRESS®
A DIVISION OF THOMAS NELSON
& ZONDERVAN

TABLE OF CONTENTS

FOREWORD v

AUTHOR'S PREFACE vi

CHAPTER 1 - PICTURE THIS 1

CHAPTER 2 - TRADITONAL AFRICAN WORLD VIEW 5

CHAPTER 3 - PRESUPPOSITIONS OF THE AFRICAN WORLD VIEW 6

CHAPTER 4 - IMPLICATIONS OF THIS WORLDVIEW 8

CHAPTER 5 - KASONGO'S CHANGE OF WORLDVIEW 10

CHAPTER 6 - A BIBLICAL WORLDVIEW 14

CHAPTER 7 - HOW TO CHANGE A WORLDVIEW 22

CHAPTER 8 - INTERMINABLE SOCIAL CONFLICTS AND AN INCREASE OF STD'S AND AIDS 28

CHAPTER 9 - CANNIBALISM 33

CHAPTER 10 - REACTIONS TO THIS MESSAGE 35

CHAPTER 11 - WHAT GOD REQUIRES TO BRING TRANSFORMATION TO A NATION 38

CHAPTER 12 - HOW GOD ACTS TO BRING TRANSFORMATION TO A NATION 43

BIBLIOGRAPHY 45

ABOUT THE AUTHOR 47

FOREWORD

"How many new churches have been started in your district during the past few years?" Such was the question I asked in a Church Growth Class I was teaching. A young man sat before me. I had taught him several years before when he had gone through the Bachelor of Divinity degree to become a pastor within the United Methodist Church. He was a good student, but I had no idea how God would use him. Now several years later, he was again in my classes this time for a further degree. He had served in the pastorate and for the last four years had been a District Superintendent. After a few seconds of reflection, he answered, "As near as I can figure, we have started eighty new churches in the last four years." I began to wonder who should be teaching the Church Growth Class. I had the theory, but Kasongo Munza had done it.

Indeed, it is a rare privilege to have a student, a friend and a colleague who takes what you give him and with God's leading develops and implements it beyond your broadest imagination. In the end, you become the student. Such is the case with Kasongo.

The horrific problems of Africa are well known. War, AIDS, disease and underdevelopment are but a few. Conferences are held at every level each year to address these enormous difficulties. The results most often have been quite disappointing. Kasongo brings a whole new fresh approach to these issues. He has taken worldview theory and applied it to the African setting. In a bold and honest way he evaluates African culture in general and his Luba culture in particular in the light of the Good News of the Kingdom of God. Kasongo's analysis starts us on the road to consider how particular aspects of a worldview may be part of the problem and stand in the way of the solutions.

He challenges us to take the reign of God as the foundation of a new worldview. The result would call for changes in our cultural worldview that are not in harmony with God's will and detrimental to progress.

While Kasongo's work and book is addressing the African milieu, its application is much larger. For those of us who work in Africa, it gives us fresh insight in how to bring the Good News of Jesus Christ in a realistic way to a people so loved by God. For those whose frame of reference is outside of Africa, the model set forth in this volume is a good one to evaluate and challenge your own cultural worldview and thinking.

I invite you to sit at the feet of my former student and join me in once again becoming his student.

Dr. David N. Persons
Dean of Faculté Méthodiste de Théologie
Mulungwishi, D.R. Congo

January 2005

AUTHOR'S PREFACE

Dear Friend,

As the New Testament makes abundantly clear, the mission of Jesus upon this earth was to proclaim to one and all the Good News that the Kingdom of God had come. As the old saying goes, "The medium is the message," so also the Gospel of John tells us that "the word became flesh and dwelt among us." Jesus not only preached the Kingdom of God, he embodied it. His message in word and deed is nothing less than a description of reality. This is what God created us to be. This is the road by which we discover the abundant life of which Jesus spoke. Jesus used many metaphors to help people see the enormity and significance of what he had brought them. One picture is of an impoverished peasant worker who, while working in the field, discovers a treasure. He sells all that he has to buy that field, but of course the loss is nothing in comparison to what he gains.

In this letter I've shared with you the significance of the Kingdom of God as a worldview with wonderful positive contributions to make to the troubled societies of Africa. However it is much more than that. It is God's answer to all societies. Like the peasant worker in the story, finding the Kingdom of God requires for everyone to abandon values and behaviors which simply are out of harmony with God's revelation of what constitutes life, given to us in Jesus Christ. In order to participate in God's ultimate gift, Africa and every other society must hold up the standard of what the Kingdom of God looks like. Anything that does not correspond must be abandoned. This loss, though it may be painful at the time, is not a loss of anything of value. It is in fact a loss of the very things that cause the most pain, distress, and hopelessness within the society. It is to lose the fetters which bind and keep people from being free.

Another picture that Jesus gives us concerning the Kingdom of God is that it starts like a tiny mustard seed, but grows into a significant tree with a great impact on its surroundings. In the same way the Kingdom of God is a worldview which, if understood, begins to change both individuals and their society. As these changes escalate the impact becomes greater and greater and can be world changing. People discover the Kingdom of God in one area of life and soon find that it impacts everything they do and say.

It is my hope that as you read this letter you will come to understand the wonderful implications which God's message in Jesus Christ conveys to Africa. It is also my prayer that this exercise of applying the template of the Kingdom of God to African society will serve as an example of how this template can be applied to all societies and situations. Thus the understanding of the Kingdom of God can grow until it fills the whole earth.

This letter is not intended to be just an academic exercise to explain the ills which afflict Africa. It is my hope that these same probing questions which are applied to African society can be applied to our individual lives. It is my prayer that as you read this letter you will allow God to bring your life into harmony with His Kingdom and be transformed into the leaven of which Jesus spoke which impacts and changes everything around it.

KASONGO MUNZA
2005

CHAPTER 1 - PICTURE THIS

Sometimes pictures say it all. Sometimes they raise questions. I want to start with some pictures that did both of these things for me.

This NASA picture is a composite of satellite photographs of the earth taken at night. I first saw it in TIME where it was an ad for Eskom, the South African electric company. (Picture NASA Earth City Lights 1994) It shows the continents of earth as they look from outer space in the dark. All of the continents are covered with lights and population centers that are bright, except Africa. To me this picture demonstrates many of the issues of Africa. The lack of lights symbolizes no electricity, which means no development and a low level of technology. Not having electricity means that work is done manually and in a primitive manner. It means communication is hampered and people are isolated. The picture makes me ask, "WHY?" Why does even Australia with its sparse population have more lights than Africa?

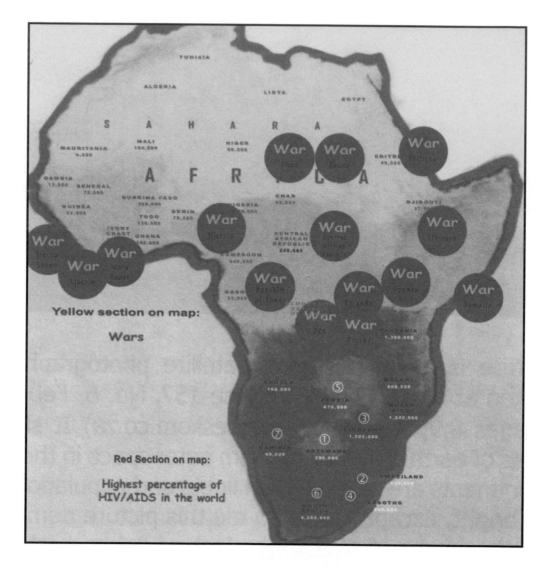

The second picture shows Africa in two colors—yellow and red. (TIME, Volume 157, No. 6, February 12, 2001, pages 48, 49) The purpose of the picture is to show the areas that have the highest concentration of HIV AIDS in the world. That is the red portion of the map. It also unintentionally shows something else. When we indicate the areas in Africa that have armed conflicts with red circles, they form a band across the widest part of the continent and all in the yellow area.

To me this is Africa bathed in blood. When I first saw this picture it struck me that the yellow portion indicates the areas of the continent that have a predominantly patriarchal culture and the portion in red has a matriarchal influence to their cultures. I had just moved from my traditionally patriarchal culture to work in a country that had strong matrilinial influence and the implication of this were reinforced for me. I'll discuss this later in this booklet.

I came across a third picture—again a map. It showed the worldwide rate of AIDS. The shocking thing for me was the disproportionate number of cases in central and southern Africa. The map used a little human figure to represent 10,000 individuals who are HIV positive. North America had four figures. South America had five. Europe had three and Northern Africa had two. In Southern Africa the number of figures could not begin to fit on the land. It formed a checkerboard that spread into the oceans on both sides of the land. I counted and there were seventy figures.

Northern Africa is predominantly Muslim while southern Africa is supposed to be 'Christian'. One of the questions that I have been struggling with is, "Why is it that the countries that are 'Christian' have this holocaust, and the Muslim countries have less than the rest of the world? Is the Gospel preached in Africa different from the Gospel preached in the rest of the world?"

REASONS PEOPLE GIVE

As I worked through these questions and discussed them with many people the reasons they gave were widely varied.

One reason given was the impact of the white man on Africa—the slave trade, which took the best from the continent; colonialism, which drained the continent of resources and gave nothing in return; and exploitation, which continues to do that.

Another reason was religious. Some believe that Africa is cursed. This can either be interpreted as the curse of Cain or the curse of Ham. Where I come from, we sometimes call ourselves the children of Eve, whereas white people are the children of Mary.

A third reason was the lack of education. If we could just educate Africans they would progress and change.

A fourth reason was our poverty. We say that poverty is the mother of all sins. It exacerbates all the other problems. If poverty is the mother of all sins, her children are crime, prostitution, superstitious activities, alcoholism, and drug abuse.

MEDICAL COMPARISON

The more I thought and prayed about this, the stronger became my conviction that all of the issues people brought up were only symptoms of a deeper disease or disorder. The AIDS pandemic, the poverty, the lack of development, the wars, the ethnic conflicts are opportunistic infections of the continent that preyed easily and at will on us because of an underlying disease. The condition of the continent is strikingly similar to the disease of AIDS.

The diseases associated with AIDS become lethal because a virus has entered the body and weakened and destroyed the immune system. It allows other infections to enter the body with ease and work havoc. So people technically do not die of AIDS. They die of malaria, TB, pneumonia, diarrhea, or any number of other ailments that should be able to be treated or fought off. But the body has no defenses, so the opportunistic infection conquers.

I have become convinced that the "virus" that has entered our continent and makes us prey to these many disasters is rooted in our worldview. There are aspects of our worldview that impede our ability to deal with the disorders that afflict our society. All the "reasons" listed above that people gave me are just opportunistic infections in our society that we have no defense against because of an inflexible worldview that damages our ability to deal with cultural diseases.

I would like to approach this by first explaining the traditional African worldview, which is a worldview I held and which had been taught to me by my parents. Then I will attempt to describe God's worldview, and share how I came to hold this.

Finally, I want to begin a discussion on how we Africans can transform our worldview. But first we must understand what a worldview is.

WHAT IS A WORLDVIEW?

The dictionary (Webster's New World College Dictionary, 1999, Page 1650) defines worldview as: "A comprehensive, especially personal, philosophy or conception of the world and of human life." Every culture has its own worldview. It is usually not something a person goes around thinking about. Worldview is assumed and subconscious.

I compare a worldview to putting on a pair of colored glasses. Some sunglasses are pinkish in color, some are green and some are brown. When a person wears one of these their view of the world seems normal to them, and only changes when they remove one set of glasses and exchange them for another color.

Cultures are a result of their respective worldviews. Worldview helps the individual deal with life within his culture. A worldview governs society at a subconscious level even more powerfully than laws and legislature. It is the reason behind conscience. Worldview can be likened to a culture's immune system. It enables a culture to determine what is harmful and what is beneficial, and it protects the society from the harmful.

For example, long ago in my culture, people had to deal with what to do about widows. The traditions that developed for assisting widows was to have the widow be taken as another wife by the eldest surviving brother of the deceased. This ensured that she was cared for and that the children remained with the family of the deceased. Many other traditions developed out of this, which I will discuss later. These motives were good for the past.

However, now things have changed and the tradition and its attending practices is now a prime means for transmitting AIDS. Because our worldview is often hidden from our conscious perception, we as Africans have a difficult time changing a tradition, even if it is harmful. It is difficult for other cultures (i.e., American, European) to understand why Africans would cling to a tradition that is harmful, and it is difficult for Africans to question that same tradition.

CHAPTER 2 - TRADITONAL AFRICAN WORLD VIEW

A worldview is usually not something that is deliberately taught, it is simply a way of living. Our African worldview is absorbed. At nights we would have competitions in story telling that also taught traditional African values and worldview.

When I was growing up within the Luba tribe my father was a chief, and he carefully instructed me in the traditions of my culture. Although he repeatedly told me that he was sending me to the white man's school, he wanted me never to forget the misumba. (The word means literally the hunting or fishing camps that one occupies temporarily.) He wanted me to learn what I needed in order to make it in the world.

"Misumba ibidi hatanda, wasatwe keuyukene." Is a proverb which means, "There are two camps in the world, but the third is unknown."

In the understanding of ancestral beliefs, there are two camps and one home in which a person experiences existence. The first camp is the mother's womb. The second camp is this world as we know it. And the third existence is the mysterious life after death and is not a camp, but is our home.

This view is cyclical in the sense that one may stay at home, but from time to time one may need to leave home to go to the camps. This cyclical worldview is repetitive.

I have diagrammed the African worldview.

African Worldview

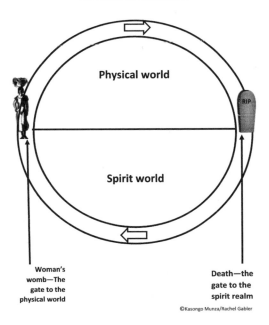

©Kasongo Munza/Rachel Gabler

How did we get this worldview? My father pointed out that the grass dies or is burned and then comes up again when the rains start. The sun disappears every evening and then reappears the next morning. Nature is cyclical, and so are our lives.

CHAPTER 3 - PRESUPPOSITIONS OF THE AFRICAN WORLD VIEW

There are many things this worldview presupposes. I will list some of the ones I am aware of.

A. Life is cyclical. (See diagram on previous page.)
  1. Half of life is visible and the other is invisible and mysterious.
  2. There are two spheres of existence—one is physical and the other is spiritual.
  3. There are two temporary places—the womb and this world.
  4. There is one place of residence—the afterlife or spirit life.

B. There are two gates to transition between the two spheres: the woman--her womb leads from spirit life to the physical life, and death--leads from physical life back to spirit life and the place of residence. The understanding of two gates leads to many rites and rituals dealing with both gates.
  1. At the first gate, pregnancy and birth, we have taboos and customs such as:
    a. Dietary taboos. (Each tribe has its own set of taboos.)
    b. "Kuputa dimi," which literally means, "to cover the pregnancy". (No one is allowed to talk about the pregnancy until the ceremony of Kuputa dimi is done at around four months.)
    c. Sterility and impotency are curses because pregnancy is impossible because the gate is closed.

  2. At the second gate, death, there are many rituals, depending on the status of the person and the manner of his/her death.
    a. The status could be an ordinary person, a king, a chief, a twin, a fool, a childless person, a leper, and an epileptic.
    b. The manner of death that would require special rituals could be suicide, a pregnant woman, and a baby dying in childbirth, a miscarriage.

C. Because of these beliefs, the logical conclusion is that there is reincarnation.
  1. Those who have died may come back and every birth is someone coming back.
  2. That is why we don't have family names; we use the names of the people who are reincarnated. The same names are used over and over.
  3. The means of determining the person who is being reincarnated are usually dreams and visions by family members during the pregnancy.
  4. When the dreams or visions do not show clearly the right identity of the one being reincarnated, people consult the diviners.

D. In our world there is interaction between the two spheres of existence—spiritual and physical.
  1. The spiritual beings possess omnipotence, omnipresence, and omniscience.
  2. The physical beings are dependent on, and subject to the spiritual beings.

3. The spiritual beings are the source of everything good or evil that happens in the physical sphere (i.e. health or disease, accidents, fertility or sterility, blessings or curses, success or failure)

E. There is intercommunication between the two spheres, the main means being dreams, visions, and signs.
   1. Dreams, visions, signs, and the use of mediums/ diviners (comparable with the prophets in Scripture) are a means for the spiritual to communicate with the physical.
   2. Invocation, sacrifices, prayers, and consultation with the mediums/ diviners are the acts of the physical communicating with the spiritual.
   3. There are good mediums who intervene on behalf of the humans: Diviners (bilumbu or ba bwanavidye), Healers (Bangaga), Priests (Bitobo).
   4. There are evil mediums: Witches (Bamfwishi) with ability to communicate with evil spirits to harm humans.

F. Harmony must be maintained among the living ones and the dead ones. Everyone is required to fulfill certain responsibilities in order to maintain harmony.
   1. Honor—never let a family member or spiritual being be dishonored.
   2. Solidarity—assist each other in any event.
   3. Sharing—property, position and benefits.
   4. Preservation of ancestral heritage—land, power and traditions—they are not negotiable.

This is the worldview that rules the lives of most of Africa. This is what I was taught as I grew up. This teaching is mostly informal. Family and friends lay it down in our subconscious while we are still infants, and it is reinforced daily. We take it in with our mother's milk.

CHAPTER 4 - IMPLICATIONS OF THIS WORLDVIEW

The implications of this worldview are profound. They affect all aspects of life.

Lack of Development:

The perception that this world is a musumba (singular of misumba) or a temporary place is an obstacle to development. It makes no sense to build good houses and roads in a place you will be occupying only temporarily. The concept of development is almost absent. A Kiluba proverb says, "Kishiya bashiya; Kitana batana." This means, "This is how we received it; as we received it is how we have to leave it." This includes style of life, housing, food, power, land or boundaries, and traditions. It is a taboo to try to change things.

Witchcraft in dealing with disease:

Fear of witchcraft distorts and negates the benefits of science and medicine. Belief that spiritual beings are the source of everything good or bad that happens in life means that all diseases are caused by these spiritual beings—including HIV/AIDS. We are not satisfied with scientific medical treatment because we "KNOW" there is someone behind the disease who is causing it. It cannot be satisfactorily treated with medicine.

Because someone or something else causes everything, there is little sense of responsibility or ability to change things. Nothing is my fault. Everything bad that happens to me, happens either because someone bewitched me, or because the spirits predestined it. This affects both development and disease management.

Fatalism:

"Kebidi ntelo biya, bidi kwabilwa na Leza," is a saying that means, "It is not because of your skills in putting traps that you are successful, it is a gift from God." Western theology might say this sounds good, but the African application of this has not been helpful. This has been interpreted to mean that you do not have to work at being skillful; you need to use fetishes to succeed.

This is why we wear and use fetishes. There are fetishes for success in school and business, for love in marriage, for security or protection against any action of one's enemies; and the list goes on.

The sacredness of ancestral heritage:

Ancestral heritage includes mainly the land and the power and traditions. These are sacred. There is no way to accept sharing land or power with other people. Land boundaries must not be changed. Democracy and rights of other tribes or people are irrelevant. It is an unforgivable sin to compromise in this area. The Kiluba proverb quoted before, "Kishiya bashiya; Kitana batana," (Which means, "This is how we received it; as we received it is how we have to leave it.") is also referring to unacceptable transfer of these resources. Colonialism changed boundaries and transferred people groups. This is why Africa has the interminable conflicts and genocide that it does, because now more than one tribe may be occupying the same land. This is discussed further in another chapter.

Sharing benefits with your relatives:

"Udya ngombe, udya na bobe; utala ngombe wakahwile!" means, "When you get meat, share it with your family, or you will not have someone to share with you when you don't have meat." It talks about not being selfish. We have had the tradition of sharing in our culture. This is a good thing.

However this sharing has been expanded to mean power or benefits if one has any social or political position. It involves much more than sharing food or goods or taking care of family. It means that if you have the office of President or Bishop or District Superintendent or Pastor you must fill the key positions around you with family members or tribal members. Churches and conferences only want fellow tribesmen or family members to have power. Qualifications and ability and character are non-issues in this matter.

This is problematic for democratic elections. You can only vote for the candidate who is most closely related to you. This is why so-called African democracies are really "tribocracies". The candidate who is a member of the largest tribe wins, and then distributes benefits to his family or tribal members.

There are two more results of these presuppositions I will mention at this point. However, they merit more discussion than this section has allowed. Therefore I am devoting a chapter to these two. They are:

Interminable social conflicts and an increase of STD's and AIDS: Chapter 8
And
Cannibalism: Chapter 9

CHAPTER 5 - KASONGO'S CHANGE OF WORLDVIEW

The event that caused me to question this worldview and began my search for the truth was the death of my father. I was very close to him and considered him my friend as well as parent. At that point I was a skeptic. As a result of my education and personal observation I no longer wanted to accept the African worldview. I had studied philosophy and had come to doubt all beliefs.

God used my father's death to make me begin to ask myself, "What really happens after death?" "How can we know?" "Is death the end or is there an afterlife?"

My wife was a Christian and had a Bible. One day I was out of reading material, and I wanted something to read. I picked up her Bible and I opened to John 14. I started with verse one.

> *"Don't be troubled. You trust God, now trust in me. There are many rooms in my Father's home, and I am going to prepare a place for you. If this were not so, I would tell you plainly. When everything is ready, I will come and get you, so that you will always be with me where I am. And you know where I am going and how to get there." "No, we don't know, Lord." Thomas said. "We haven't any idea where you are going so how can we know the way?" Jesus told him, "I am the way, the truth, and the life. No one can come to the Father except through me."* John 14: 1-6 NIV

These verses were like a light being switched on in a dark room. Here were the answers I was looking for:

A. A man had come from God to tell us what happens after death.
1. His origin—heaven
2. His person—He is God the creator
3. His mission—to show us the way to the Father

B. His message to us—He says that there is an afterlife. This world is not our place of residence, that world is. He has come to show us the way to that place, the truth about it, and to give eternal life.
C. The reason for our presence in this world--Jesus Christ affirms some of the presuppositions of the African worldview and corrects others.
D. There are two spheres of existence--this life and the afterlife.
1. This world is not our home. It is our place of assignment. Our home is with our Heavenly Father.
2. Although this world is not our home, we are responsible for its condition. We need to improve it and take care of it.
3. The gate to our home is not death, but Jesus Christ. We pass through this gate when we believe in Him. (John10:9) Our eternal life begins at this point.

"I am the door. If anyone enters by Me, he will be saved, and will go in and out and find pasture." John 10:9 NKJV

E. Death is the end of physical life, but spiritual life continues with God.

F. When we learn what ghosts are, we learn we don't need to fear them.
1. Life is not cyclical.
2. Reincarnation: There is no return to this life after death. (Luke 16: 19-31, Hebrews 9:2)
3. What ghosts are and that we don't need to fear them.

"There was a certain rich man who was clothed in purple and fine linen and fared sumptuously every day. "But there was a certain beggar named Lazarus, full of sores, who was laid at his gate, desiring to be fed with the crumbs which fell from the rich man's table. Moreover the dogs came and licked his sores.

"So it was that the beggar died, and was carried by the angels to Abraham's bosom. The rich man also died and was buried. And being in torments in Hades, he lifted up his eyes and saw Abraham afar off, and Lazarus in his bosom.

"Then he cried and said, 'Father Abraham, have mercy on me, and send Lazarus that he may dip the tip of his finger in water and cool my tongue; for I am tormented in this flame.'

"But Abraham said, 'Son, remember that in your lifetime you received your good things, and likewise Lazarus evil things; but now he is comforted and you are tormented. 'And besides all this, between us and you there is a great gulf fixed, so that those who want to pass from here to you cannot, nor can those from there pass to us.'

"Then he said, 'I beg you therefore, father, that you would send him to my father's house, for I have five brothers, that he may testify to them, lest they also come to this place of torment.'

"Abraham said to him, 'They have Moses and the prophets; let them hear them.'

"And he said, 'No, father Abraham; but if one goes to them from the dead, they will repent.'

"But he said to him, 'If they do not hear Moses and the prophets, neither will they be persuaded though one rise from the dead.'" Luke 16:19-31 NKJV

And as it is appointed for men to die once, but after this the judgment. Hebrews 9:27 KJV

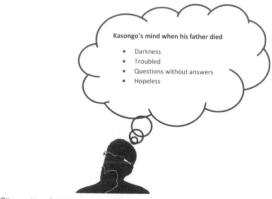

©Kasongo Munza/Rachel Gabler

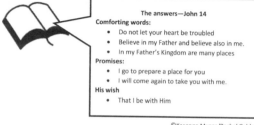

©Kasongo Munza/Rachel Gabler

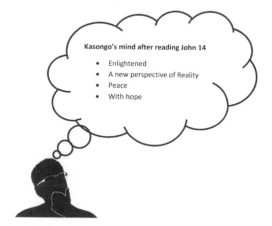

©Kasongo Munza/Rachel Gabler

This was the answer I was searching for.

Our real home—Heaven not "misumba.

Our real Father—God, our Heavenly Father

Our passage home—Jesus not death—He is the way

Death—Nothing to fear—it is the time/place of transition between the physical world and the spiritual world.

Our presence in this misumba—It is for a purpose. There is a mission or task for each one of us.

As the Father has sent me, I also send you. John 20:21 NKJV

I now had:
Trust
Hope
Joy
Peace
Love
Faith
A calling

My call is almost a compulsion. I have to reveal to my fellow Africans and Westerners the real provision of hope for Africa and the world. I am convinced that it is a true perception of the world.

Light: Wow! Now I see!
Answers: Now I know!
What a wonderful:
Hope!
Peace!
Joy!
Love!

My passion is to lift up this light the Lord has shown me to my fellow Africans!

CHAPTER 6 - A BIBLICAL WORLDVIEW

I have drawn a visual diagram of a Biblical Worldview. (Of course, there are many Biblical references, and some of these are listed by chapter and verse. The verses are then printed out at the end of this chapter for reference.)

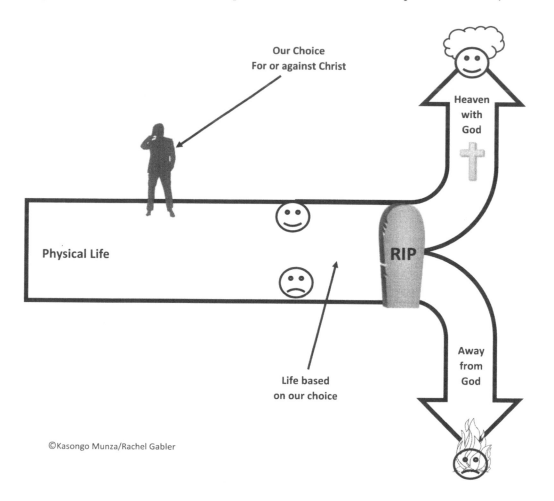

©Kasongo Munza/Rachel Gabler

Physical life:

We are all born with physical life. All human beings experience this. What makes humans different from animals is that they have a spiritual existence and the possibility of a spiritual life, determined by a choice they make at some point in their physical life.

Our choice:

We are born with a free choice to make: We can live our lives with or without God.

Our life based on this choice:

With God:

- Our life with God begins the moment we believe Christ died for our sins.
- God the Holy Spirit is with us and never leaves us from that moment.
- Physical life ends on earth; the soul with spiritual life continues for eternity in heaven.

Without God:

- We try to manage our own lives without God's help.
- Satan owns us.
- Physical life ends on earth; the soul without spiritual life is separated eternally from God.

Death for the person with God:

- Our real home is heaven.
- The way home is Jesus
- Death is the separation between the things of heaven and the things of earth. (II Corinthians 5:8, Revelation 14:13)

Death for the person without God:

- When life ends, it is eternal death.
- This person has no home, only a destination.
- There is no way to change his or her mind or return after death
- There is eternal separation from God

If we believe and accept the Biblical worldview, then:

- Attempts to communicate with dead persons are nonsense. (Parable of Lazarus the beggar: Luke 16:19-30)
- Fear of ghosts is nonsense.
- Our African practice of all kinds of rituals (having to do with twins, funerals, cleansing, etc.) is useless.
- The power of witchcraft is broken.

THE SPIRITUAL WORLD

God's Word and worldview have the answers to the hold the spirit-world has on us. Again, I have diagrammed this. We have two levels.

©Kasongo Munza/Rachel Gabler

LEVEL ONE: **God**

 God is the ONLY creator of everything
 He is symbolized by a triangle
  - He is a trinity of Father, Son and Holy Spirit
  - He is a unity where each person of the trinity has:
   * Omnipresence (present every where at all times)
   * Omniscience (knows everything)
   * Omnipotence (has all power)

LEVEL TWO: **The Angels**

Are spiritual beings (Hebrews 1:6)
Are created beings—created by God (Nehemiah 9:6; Colossians 1:16)
Were created for God's glory and purpose (Philippians 2:9-11)
Are not God and do not have His nature or power (Colossians 12:18)

One group is fulfilling their purpose which is:
- To serve God (Psalms 103:20-21)
- To worship God (Colossians 1:16)
- To assist others (us included) in their service and worship of God (Hebrews 1:14)
- Are innumerable (Job 25:3; Hebrews 12: 22)
- Have a hierarchy (Revelation 12:7; I Peter 3:22)

The other group went in opposition to God their creator;
- Satan is the leader
- His position was the former chief commandant of God's army
- His goal is overturning God's ownership and leadership (Ezekiel 28:15-17; 14:12-14)
- His tactics are like any African opposition group in rebellion.
    * Blinding people's minds/intelligence (II Cor. 4:4)
    * Infiltrating his brilliant agents in key sciences, which rule the world in order to bring confusion, doubt, divisions, tragedies (Matthew 13:24; II Corinthians 11:13-15)
    * Manipulating all kinds of both human and spiritual beings for the battle (Ephesians 6:12)
    * Falsely accusing (Job 1:7; 2:2; Genesis 3:1; II Corinthians 11:3)
    * Seducing key men and women of the world with power, money and sex, which leads to dictatorships, corruption, promiscuity, crime

Because God is all powerful, all knowing and everywhere present, the tactics of Satan will not be able to overcome God's people if they rely on Him.

Fellow Africans, there are very sophisticated satanic traps that still keep Africa in darkness and blood. Believe me, there is hope for Africa. I see it shining, but who will lift up the Light of the Lord? Who will stand up with the Lord's truth that sets everyone free?

I have referred to God's worldview as a light – similar to what happened to the Apostle Paul on his way to Damascus. A sudden light stopped him and what he was planning to do. Or it is like the prophets in the Old Testament and their visions.

God's worldview is something really simple and at the same time difficult to explain. It can be compared to a road map.

GOD'S ROAD MAP

I am aware that the example of a road map will be difficult for most Africans to understand who have not traveled overseas or in a country like South Africa. In most of Africa we get our directions from an individual who knows the location. However, I am writing this to all Africans, and there are many to whom this will make sense.

A road map is a book, which contains all the necessary information about the area you are traveling in. It has the location where you are, the location of your destination, and the distances to locations, and even may have the duration of the trip and expected fuel consumption. There are paper road maps and electronic road maps and internet road maps.

If you are moving around in a city, you need one of these in your car and you need to be able to read it. Only a foolish person would not have one, unless they already knew the city very well.

For cultures, their worldview is their map. However, for us Africans, the world has changed around us. Things that used to be simple no longer apply. Our map has gotten wrinkled, torn and smudged. We have misinterpreted it and there are buildings and obstacles that are not indicated on our map. We could take the Western map and try to drive our lives by that. However, when one looks at the direction Western countries are going, I, for one, do not like that map. It is also wrinkled, torn and smudged, as well as stained with blood.

God has given us a life road map. Even though the world around us changes, His road map safely navigates us. It has all we need to know to be able to drive our lives safely, and confidently. He has room on His highways for Africans, Europeans, American, Indians, Chinese, and every other culture. His map works for all of them, and it can be used as a guide within each distinctive culture.

Do we want to know God's directions for marriage? How about sex? How about church leadership? How about health and sickness? How about food? How about clothing? God's Word speaks to all of these issues and many more.

The question is, do we want to go God's way, or do we want our own way? To seek God's directions, God's path, we consult His road map. If we just have a vague idea of what His directions are, we will get lost. We need to pick up the map and study it. We need to make our itinerary and then stick to the directions. If we wander off the route God has prescribed, we cannot blame God when we get lost.

This applies to our individual lives, our churches, our communities, our countries and our continent. Which map are we following?

References: NKJV

II Corinthians 5:8 *We are confident, yes, well pleased rather to be absent from the body and to be present with the Lord.*

Revelation 14:13 *Then I heard a voice from heaven saying to me, "Write: 'Blessed are the dead who die in the Lord from now on.'" "Yes," says the Spirit, "that they may rest from their labors, and their works follow them."*

Nehemiah 9:6 *You alone are the LORD; You have made heaven, The heaven of heavens, with all their host, The earth and everything on it, The seas and all that is in them, And You preserve them all. The host of heaven worships You.*

Colossians 1:16 *For by Him all things were created that are in heaven and that are on earth, visible and invisible, whether thrones or dominions or principalities or powers. All things were created through Him and for Him.*

Philippians 2:9-11 *Therefore God also has highly exalted Him and given Him the name which is above every name, that at the name of Jesus every knee should bow, of those in heaven, and of those on earth, and of those under the earth, and that every tongue should confess that Jesus Christ is Lord, to the glory of God the Father.*

Hebrews 1:6 *But when He again brings the firstborn into the world, He says: "Let all the angels of God worship Him."*

Colossians 2:18 *Let no one cheat you of your reward, taking delight in false humility and worship of angels, intruding into those things which he has not seen, vainly puffed up by his fleshly mind,*

Psalms 103:20-21 *Bless the LORD, you His angels, Who excel in strength, who do His word, Heeding the voice of His word. Bless the LORD, all you His hosts, You ministers of His, who do His pleasure.*

Colossians 1:16 *For by Him all things were created that are in heaven and that are on earth, visible and invisible, whether thrones or dominions or principalities or powers. All things were created through Him and for Him.*

Hebrews 1:14 *Are they not all ministering spirits sent forth to minister for those who will inherit salvation?*

Job 25:3 *Is there any number to His armies? Upon whom does His light not rise?*

Hebrews 12: 22 *But you have come to Mount Zion and to the city of the living God, the heavenly Jerusalem, to an innumerable company of angels,*

Revelation 12:7 *And war broke out in heaven: Michael and his angels fought with the dragon; and the dragon and his angels fought,*

I Peter 3:22 *who has gone into heaven and is at the right hand of God, angels and authorities and powers having been made subject to Him.*

Ezekiel 28:15 and 17 *Thou wast perfect in thy ways from the day that thou wast created, till iniquity was found in thee... Thine heart was lifted up because of thy beauty, thou hast corrupted thy wisdom by reason of thy brightness: I will cast thee to the ground, I will lay thee before kings, that they may behold thee.*

II Corinthians 4:4 *Whose minds the god of this age has blinded, who do not believe, lest the light of the gospel of the glory of Christ, who is the image of God, should shine on them.*

Matthew 13:24-30 *Another parable He put forth to them, saying: "The kingdom of heaven is like a man who sowed good seed in his field; "but while men slept, his enemy came and sowed tares among the wheat and went his way. "But when the grain had sprouted and produced a crop, then the tares also appeared.*

So the servants of the owner came and said to him, 'Sir, did you not sow good seed in your field? How then does it have tares?'

"He said to them, 'An enemy has done this.' The servants said to him, 'Do you want us then to go and gather them up?'

"But he said, 'No, lest while you gather up the tares you also uproot the wheat with them. 'Let both grow together until the harvest, and at the time of harvest I will say to the reapers, "First gather together the tares and bind them in bundles to burn them, but gather the wheat into my barn."'

II Corinthians 11:13-15 *For such are false apostles, deceitful workers, transforming themselves into apostles of Christ. And no wonder! For Satan himself transforms himself into an angel of light.*

Therefore it is no great thing if his ministers also transform themselves into ministers of righteousness, whose end will be according to their works.

Ephesians 6:12 *For we do not wrestle against flesh and blood, but against principalities, against powers, against the rulers of the darkness of this age, against spiritual hosts of wickedness in the heavenly places.*

Job 1:9-10 *So Satan answered the LORD and said, "Does Job fear God for nothing? Have You not made a hedge around him, around his household, and around all that he has on every side? You have blessed the work of his hands, and his possessions have increased in the land.*

Genesis 3:1 *Now the serpent was more cunning than any beast of the field which the LORD God had made. And he said to the woman, "Has God indeed said, 'You shall not eat of every tree of the garden'?"*

II Corinthians 11:3 *But I fear, lest somehow, as the serpent deceived Eve by his craftiness, so your minds may be corrupted from the simplicity that is in Christ.*

CHAPTER 7 - HOW TO CHANGE A WORLDVIEW

I know from experience that changing a worldview is not an easy thing to do. I have been in a real struggle over this. At one time I was about to give up and forget it. But God is good—all the time. When He assigns you a task, you can be sure He will also provide for the means and the way to do it.

The Lord led me to use the approach He used when He was on earth and needed to explain a concept that seemed difficult for the people to understand—a parable. The parable He led me to was the parable of the barren fig tree in Luke 13:6-9. Fig trees are not well known by most Africans, but I was living in the middle of a banana plantation and saw a wide variety of productiveness in banana plants. So let me tell you the "Parable of the Banana Plant."

> He also spoke this parable: *"A certain man had a fig tree planted in his vineyard, and he came seeking fruit on it and found none. "Then he said to the keeper of his vineyard, 'Look, for three years I have come seeking fruit on this fig tree and find none. Cut it down; why does it use up the ground?'*
>
> *"But he answered and said to him, 'Sir, let it alone this year also, until I dig around it and fertilize it. 'And if it bears fruit, well. But if not, after that you can cut it down.'"* Luke 13:6-9 NKJV

Fig trees are not well known by most Africans, but I was living in the middle of a banana plantation and saw a wide variety of productiveness in banana plants. So, let me tell you the "Parable of the Banana Plant".

We have here two pictures. The first is of a stalk of bananas from the locally grown plant. The second is of two stalks from our Kafakumba bananas.

I would like to tell you about these.

These plants were both grown at the same location. They had the same soil, the same climate, the same conditions and they were planted in the same season—one by the father and the others by his son—essentially the same planters.

We see that there is a big difference in the stalks. One is very tiny and one is large. Why?

This is not hard to figure out. Since two white men planted them, no one will blame this on witchcraft. One is not cursed by the devil or God. There is no invisible power at work here. When you look at the preparation and care the plants received, you see the reason for the differences (Luke 13:6-9). It becomes obvious that when growing a banana plantation there are some actions that need to be taken in order to make a difference.

So it is with Africa. The problem is not the continent. The problem is the ground, and the ground is the worldview that Africa has been rooted in and the lack of an enlightened planter (Romans 10:2). Development does not just happen. It is the fruit of a long series of actions taken at the right time by the right people. In other words, if we really want to change the picture of Africa, some actions must be carefully taken.

BANANA DEVELOPMENT

Let me describe the action to be taken to change our worldview in terms of our banana cultivation.

Any planter knows you cannot plant in the bush or forest. Nothing will grow unless the bush is cleared. The steps to be taken to prepare for a plantation are as follows:

23

TASK #1 CLEARING THE GROUND

This part involves clearing and what we call stumping. It is not enough to chop the trees down—their stumps and roots must be dug out. Otherwise the stumps will obstruct the proper planting of the small banana plants and the roots will cause the same vegetation to grow back.

Stumping consists of uprooting trees. The aim of this action is to clear out all kinds of obstacles to the growth of the plant. Africa is a forest. It is a big forest of mysteries and taboos. Not much is known about Africa. The forest of fear blocks all attempts to know it.

Many studies have been published. But very little has been said. No one will assume the risk of talking about the untalkable, revealing the unrevealable Africa. So the most important task for the growth of Africa is to come to a decision to break all kinds of taboos and mysteries, which block the growth of our continent. The time has come to break the silence. The time for stumping mysteries, taboos, fear. God's word says, "Fear not."

Fear not, for I am with you; Be not dismayed, for I am your God. I will strengthen you, Yes, I will help you, I will uphold you with My righteous right hand.' Isaiah 41:10 NKJV

TASK #2 DIGGING

After stumping the bush, comes another major action needed for the growth of our plants. It is the work of digging out or removing earth that may contain a high level of acid that can damage our plant. So it is our task to dig out all the bad soil (wrong beliefs and practices) before planting a banana plant. This step presents two potentially fatal dangers. One consists of eradicating all behavior that seems distinctly African. This is a common trap many missionaries and other planters (colonialists) fell into. The other danger is one that Africans have tended to. It is being too proud of their culture; they fall very easily in a trap of syncretism or protectionism.

So this step must neither throw all the earth away nor must it retain all the earth regardless of its effects on the plants.

In our process of development, attention should be given to the point that Africa is not only what we see. It is not only what people can touch or hear. Africa is also what they feel. It is what they believe without knowing they believe it. This also can block the process of development. Therefore, this needs to be dug out and examined.

Digging does not necessarily mean throwing out. I am fully convinced that there are a lot of positive concepts in our culture. For instance, the concept of hospitality, solidarity, and mutual assistance—these are social values that deserve our consideration. But digging out helps us to look into the culture. Then with the Lord's light it helps us to explore, evaluate and select what is good and positive from what is negative. It also helps us to appreciate and value what we retain.

So the action of digging out is of great significance. The Bible says, *"And no one puts new wine into old wineskins; or else the new wine bursts the wineskins, the wine is spilled, and the wineskins are ruined. But new wine must be put into new wineskins."* Mark 2: 22 NKJV

TASK #3 FERTILIZING

Remember the problem is not the tree. It is the ground (the worldview) it has been rooted in. (Luke 13:6-9) After the action of digging out all the hidden concepts, the next action is fertilizing. This consists of feeding the worldview with both the Lord's social and scientific principles. (Science does not own its principles. God created science, and He owns the principles He created. Scientific principles are not exclusive to what is called science.)

We use commercial fertilizer and lots of chicken manure. You might ask why would I compare God's Biblical principles with manure? Sometimes the things God expects or requires are difficult, uncomfortable, or even shocking to us. Jesus Christ said that following him would not always be pleasant. A cross is not fun.

The methods used in applying "fertilizer and manure" need to be varied. We need to use every means available to us. Radio, television, videos, publications are tools to be used by the church and by schools that understand the purpose of this application of "fertilizer". People's minds must be reached, in a way they have never been reached to date. We must be creative and intentional in this activity. We must not be merely educating for the sake of knowledge, we must be teaching for the transformation of lives.

Transformation won't happen automatically. If we are going to be transformed, we must first see the need for this. That is why TASK # 1, CLEARING THE GROUND, is so important. Applying fertilizer indiscriminately, without clearing out what we don't want to grow will have the effect of causing anything and everything to grow. And weeds grow better and faster than useful plants, as Christ mentioned in the parable of the sower. This transformation must be in the hearts and minds of God's people.

After the fertilizer and manure are applied, the plant is placed in the hole and the good earth that remained from the evaluation of Task #3 is filled in around it. The plant now has a good start at growing. Again I say, not all the ground is bad. It may be merely nutrient-deficient and the fertilizer and manure will compensate. It may consist of stones and other material that is detrimental to proper growth. Not all of our African culture is bad. We will need to retain much of it. But it must be examined.

TASK #4 TENDING

Tending has two aspects. In banana cultivation there is the treatment part of continual application of water and fertilizer and monitoring, and then there is the preventative part of weeding and pruning the suckers. Just because a worldview has been analyzed, and the negative aspects identified and eliminated, and just because God's worldview and teachings have replaced the negative, does not mean the work is done. In fact, it is just beginning.

Weeding is a constant process. The weeds were there in task number one, but they are pernicious and will return. They will absorb the nutrients and water that the bananas need if they are allowed to remain. They will eventually take over the whole plantation if not dealt with. *And let us not grow weary while doing good, for in due season we shall reap if we do not lose heart.* (Galatians 6:9 NKJV). The negative influences and values do not go away once for all, they continually return—the Christian life is a constant process.

The plants must be watered constantly. Banana plants need lots of water. As church leaders, our source of water is the Living Water. Pastors, Lay Leaders, Sunday School Teachers all have their plantations that need the application of Living Water. The Living Water must come from these leaders themselves. John 7:38 speaks about Living Water flowing from us. Therefore we must have transformed leaders. *"He who believes in Me, as the Scripture has said, out of his heart will flow rivers of living water."* (NKJV)

These transformed leaders also have the responsibility to monitor the plantation. They must know what to look for and how to correct problems that may arise in the plants. This is why I believe in focusing on church leadership training.

It would greatly assist the preventative part of weeding and pruning if lawmakers understood this and backed the efforts here. I am speaking of having legislators on both the national and international level who will support appropriate laws against damaging practices such as rituals of cleansing of widows and widowers, unhealthy circumcision, funeral practices that disable the family, witchcraft and divination.

This fourth task takes time. It must continue during the entire life of the plant. Then when that plant bears fruit, the task continues over the next generation of plants. It never stops.

When these tasks are done consistently and with care, there is harvest. There are people and churches whose lives are changed. With God nothing is impossible!

CHAPTER 8 - INTERMINABLE SOCIAL CONFLICTS AND AN INCREASE OF STD'S AND AIDS

Diagnosis and treatment:

In this section we look at serious diseases of the continent, make a diagnosis, and prescribe treatment. We coin a word to describe the treatment. The word is "Theotherapy". This comes out of my present situation of undergoing chemotherapy. I am under treatment for non-Hodgkin's lymphoma. Chemotherapy involves using strong medication to eradicate the cancer cells. It is painful and unpleasant. It produces temporary side effects. However, in order to deal with cancer, this is necessary to endure. With "Theotherapy" we must go after and eradicate the diseases in our societies, and then healing can begin.

When looking carefully at the map showing countries affected by either war or by AIDS, it is very easy to make these observations:

- Africa has two different social zones—war zone and STD zone.
- The war zone includes specifically countries of Central and Western Africa.
- STD's (AIDS) occurs in almost all the southern part of Africa—from Zambia to South Africa.
- The war zone is a nightmare—massive killing, raping, insecurity, refugees, and a lack of any vital infrastructure. It is the area where the law of the jungle prevails.
- The STD zone is very different. It has peace, security, progress in democracy, and the existence of vital infrastructure. The negative picture of this zone consists of a tremendous increase in moral and social problems—promiscuity, instability of marriages, STD's, AIDS, orphans, street kids, drugs, poverty, criminality.

Many reasons have been suggested. Some accuse the colonial powers. Others have used as an excuse the fact that people are so poor—they are jobless, hungry, etc.

But when looking at this situation through God's worldview, it seems to me that people, through their worldview, are focusing on the symptoms instead of the disease. In fact it is the defective matrilineal system or patrilineal system characterizing a society that is the disease.

PATRIARCHAL SOCIETY

The war zone consists of male dominated societies. In other words, it is organized according to the social system called a "Patriarchal Society".

Description:

- The power and right of leadership remains exclusively with men.
- It is very rare to see a woman holding the position of chieftain.
- The man is the head and the wife the tail.

- In this type of society men behave like lions. They are very protective of their territory (land), their power and their "pride" of wives and children—quite a few wives and children if possible.
- It is not possible to share these things outside your family. (See Chapter 4) It is a sacred heritage, not open for debate or compromise or vote or negotiation. The values of the society must be protected at any cost, even if it means making a pact with Satan.
- We sing in Kiluba,

> "Kyotufwila kino i tanda!
> Kyotufwila kino i tanda
> Yashile bakambo."

> "What are we fighting for?
> We are fighting for the land
> That our ancestors handed down to us."

- The fighting that is going on is not for a leader or political party or ideology. They are fighting for "tanda".
- This fighting is leading to an AIDS pandemic on the horizon because it is being used as a weapon of mass destruction. There are divisions of soldiers who are known to be HIV positive whose function is to enter a village after fighting has come through and systematically rape the women and girls in order to infect them and thus destroy the population in the future.

Colonialism:

The impact of colonialism on the patriarchal society was to create a situation that was ready to explode when it was removed. In order to control the different groups of people the colonial powers disrupted the tribal structures and existing systems of power sharing, moved groups of people, chose leaders regardless of their tribe of origin, social status or their location. This totally disrupted the tribal structures, boundaries and the mechanisms for inheriting power that were keeping the societies at peace.

The attitude of local people during that time is well expressed through this Luba song:

> Ditungulu kotopeka Kaminwa
> Batwe bonso mu tapa ya kiluwe

It was a song about two different wild fruit that a hunter picked and put in his bag for his provision. "Kaminwa" began quarreling with "Ditungulu". Then a wise person told "Ditungulu" that it was not wise to quarrel with "Kaminwa" since they were both victims of the hunter. Better first wait and see what would happen to the hunter (colonialist) and be tolerant during this time of the hunter's power.

After the colonial era, because of the lack of adequate or appropriate political structure to help different tribes (Ditungulu and Kaminwa) live and share power together, nothing was done to solve the case of the two fruit. "Ditungulu" began to claim the restoration of their land and power left by the "hunter" to the "outsiders" (Kaminwa). The result has been interminable conflicts, genocide, refugees, insecurity, poverty, child soldiers, and the myriad of problems we see today.

Well-meaning efforts of the international community:

When looking through God's worldview, I can easily see all the mistakes the international community is making by imposing democracy. They are aware of some of the hurdles they face, and totally oblivious to others. Some of these hurdles are:

- What kind of effective program can you have when you have a gun pointed in your face?
- What is going to be your motivation to persevere when you know that what you accomplished today will be smashed and looted this evening?
- What kind of strategies are you going to set up to stop the spread of AIDS when every day thousands of innocent women and girls are being raped or turned into sex slaves?
- What hope are you going to give the men returning from war who learn that their wives are HIV positive?
- Can a Kasai "lion" live in peace with a Luba "lion" any more than a Palestinian "lion" live with a Jewish "lion" or an American "lion" live with an Iraqi "lion"?

Diagnosis:

The endemic disease in this society is the concept of land and power. People in this society believe land and power are the properties of spiritual beings, the "Mikishi". It was given to our ancestors for the sake of their people to be passed from generation to generation. Therefore, land and power have a sacred character and are inseparable—you cannot have power without land. On earth no one has authority to either share land and power, or to negotiate about it with people from other cultures or tribes. The duty of these people is to protect this heritage at any cost. Not performing these duties of preserving land and power will bring a curse on the land, the people and the next generations. That is the source of "lionism" or protective mentality.

Appropriate treatment—Theotherapy:

As the disease in this society has a spiritual dimension, any political attempt to heal it is like prescribing aspirin for cancer. The treatment of this disease needs to be spiritual. God's worldview and its application are the medication needed to treat it. In God's worldview He is the owner of everything. All power belongs to Him. He loves ALL people, all tribes. When we get to heaven, we will be sharing it with ALL tribes, and the church needs to start showing how that is done here on earth.

The part of this "Theotherapy" that will be particularly unpleasant for the church is the teaching and practicing of servant leadership. Our churches are power-hungry institutions. Our church leaders do not lead in a Christ like way. They treat their positions like African chiefdoms. The church does not demonstrate to the world anything that is different or better than what it already has. The church needs to be different from the world, not imitating it.

MATRILINEAL SOCIETY

The STD zone is basically the opposite of the War zone. It consists of basically female dominated societies—the matrilineal society.

Description:

- The land and power are not exclusively a male right. There are many female chiefs.
- People in this zone are tolerant. A form of democracy is possible, though it is still founded on tribalism.
- In this society children belong to their mother's family.
- In this sense the father does not have authority and responsibility for the children.
- Women have more power than in the Patriarchal Society, although this is limited. A woman has the say in regard to her children and her husband.
- War is NOT acceptable.
- Since by nature females are more concerned with security and survival than power and land this has many implications.
    - Promiscuity and divorce are daily events.
    - Sex is an asset to be used to survive.
    - STD's and AIDS have a green light.
    - Orphans, widows, street kids, are legion.
- Moral and social foundations are not solid.
- Negotiation and power sharing are possible.
- Poverty is a social cancer.

Well meaning efforts of the international community:

When confronting the disease in these zones, what are our chances of success when:

- The focus is only on antiretroviral drugs and condoms and orphanages?
- The church is too holy (or too bound by taboos) to speak openly on the transformation of sexual behavior?
- No attention is paid to the sandy foundations of the moral and social values of society?
- The church never speaks about the human value of women, men and children, or God's view of marriage?
- When the so-called church is an extension of tribalism?

Diagnosis:

The underlying disease in this society is the concept of woman's sex. It is perceived as a powerful tool to be used whenever, wherever and with whomever in order to obtain whatever she needs whether it is material goods, social advantages, or influence. In actuality, it shows how totally powerless women are if their only advantage is sex. When a female's value is only in the sexual relations she has, she is not viewed or valued as God views or values her. This utilitarian view of female sex has led to all kinds of sex-profitable unions. There is promiscuity, prostitution, and all forms of living together without any social form of recognition or protection. One descriptive saying in Lingala speaks of marriages that are, "Tumbula bwaka." This means, "Pick up and drop" marriages.

Appropriate treatment—Theotherapy:

Like chemotherapy, we must apply God's worldview to this type of society. It will mean eradicating the false values that the culture has placed on women and replacing it with God's value of them. It will involve radical presentation about God's teaching on sex, marriage, men, women, and children.

As you can see here, we are not talking about only getting people saved. This disease has flourished where the gospel has been preached and where most individuals would say they have been saved at some point. Zambia was declared a "Christian nation". But that is like prescribing aspirin for cancer. Though I am thankful for the church work to date, we need to be honest and accept that the church has failed to speak out openly about sex, marriage, and family. The result is that "Christian" countries are the most characterized by a high rate of promiscuity, dirty sex, broken marriages, AIDS, street kids, orphans, criminality, poverty. But better late than never, the church should draw wisdom from the French saying, "La meilleure façon de regretter les erreurs du passé, c'est de faire le present meilleur." Which means, "The best way to be remorseful for the past is to improve the present." We must start now.

We must reconstruct families and marriages. This will take coordinated effort on the part of the church. No means must be ignored. Because we need to change the foundation of this society, we must be serious about this. We must concentrate on women, and especially mothers. This is because the mothers are raising the next generation of Africans, and they hold the key.

We must teach them that God places great value on them as people. God values their daughters and their sons. God's value of them is not based on whether they have children. Christ died for them and has a plan for their lives that can change them. God's plan for sex is wonderful. It can only be wonderful when it is within the bounds of marriage. God is the inventor of sex, and we do not need to be embarrassed to say this.

The other aspect we must address is the devaluation this society places on men and husbands. Men are valued only for the income they bring in. If they aren't able to provide as well as the ones down the street, they are replaced. They are not expected to have any impact on their own children. Their responsibility to child rearing is to their sister's children, not their own. As they say, "How can I be sure my wife's children are my own? The only children I know are directly related to me are my sister's children that came from her body."

God's plan for marriage is the medicine this tragedy needs. We in the church must proclaim it.

More research needed:

I realize that these observations and conclusions are controversial. Much more study needs to be done on the correlation between the two systems (Patriarchal and Matrilineal) and the statistics of STD's and war. I also realize that I am biased in my belief that Theotherapy is the solution. However, I have seen the results of many other attempts to address the problems in Africa. I can't see that anything else has a chance.

CHAPTER 9 - CANNIBALISM

"Why do your soldiers eat pygmy meat? Is it due to the fact that you are now running out of food in your area?" This question was asked by a BBC reporter in an interview of a leader of a combatant group based in the northern part of the Democratic Republic of the Congo.

Most people, especially Westerners, think cannibalism is a matter of normal food like beef, fish, etc. being scarce. Few even want to know how prevalent it is or why it happens. We have a Luba proverb, "Wami tata kyamudile bitupu, i bwanga bwankomeshe meso." It is in our songs and traditions. It means, "I did not eat my father for no reason. It was because of the fetish (bwanga) that I was forced to."

One needs to ask oneself, how this can happen? How can a normal person come to the point of calmly eating parts of his or her relative or a fellow human being unless there is an underlying reason or purpose that would demand such an act? This subject has been and still is a matter of much speculation, most of it without knowledge of the truth of the culture. This is a huge secret in our society. I will list some of the background beliefs:

- Behind cannibalism lies a strong belief that sacrificial blood contains supernatural power.
- Levels of power vary according to the type and purpose of sacrifice.
- One level of power deals with the blood of domestic animals like chickens, cows, pigeons.
- Another level would be a wild animal such as lion, leopard, and certain bird or reptile.
- The ultimate is a human sacrifice.
- The levels also vary according to the status of the human and the reason for the sacrifice.
- Usually this goes from baby to elder.
- However, for some purposes the youngest person has more sacrificial value (power) for the fetish.
- Or, it may be the closest and most important person will give one the most power.
- The fetishes to which these sacrifices are made are endless: invincibility, invisibility, invulnerability, luck, success in business, winning an election, winning a soccer match, winning your spouse, winning the favor of your boss.
- This is being practiced, not only by non-educated people, but runs deep among the most educated social classes—our political leaders, students, business men, army officers, even church leaders.

If I were to try to give an estimate of the percent of people practicing fetish, I would not be far off in estimating 80%, and ritualistic cannibalism factors in about 10% of this 80 %. The fact is that these things remain secret and private. One might know of it, but never say a single word. African power!

When looking through God's worldview it is simple to point out some important revelations.

- There is a high level of sophisticated satanic manipulation and blindness.
- Indeed there is power in blood—but it is the Lamb of God whose blood has power.
- The blood of Christ cleanses, protects, gives victory, heals, casts out demons and evil spirits. It is all we need.
- Christianity has not taught this clearly, and the misconceptions have reinforced false African teaching.

When viewed through God's perspective, all other sacrifices are useless and the death of so many humans to provide fetish power, is an enormous tragedy.

The French say, "Il ne faut pas être prophète ou un illustre chercheur." The literal translation is, "There is no need to be a prophet or intelligent researcher." In American English you would say, " You don't need to be a rocket scientist to figure this out." The only thing you need is to be plugged into God's worldview.

CHAPTER 10 - REACTIONS TO THIS MESSAGE

Long before considering writing this booklet, the Lord brought me into contact with people from many cultures and backgrounds from all over Africa, and sparked in me a great interest in how other cultures think. It started in the beginning of my pastoral ministry. Soon after graduation from Theological University in 1980 I joined the staff of Kafakumba Pastors' School. This was in addition to my work as a pastor. This exposed me to a wide variety of cultures that came from all over D.R. Congo (then Zaire). I began investing time and energy in training pastors from many different areas of Africa. This area has grown to include in each annual session around 150 pastors from Zambia, Zimbabwe, Senegal, and Tanzania and, of course, Democratic Republic of Congo. This exposure planted in me a desire that has become a passion to look at how different people from different cultures think.

Another event that nourished this desire was when I was released to become a full time staff member of Kafakumba Training Center in Zambia. This step involved my relocation to another country and another culture (still within Africa). Now I had even more interaction with students and church leaders from other cultures. Pastors' School is two months out of the year, but now I am teaching every month and sometimes every week. I have an ideal situation to indulge this passion. Sometimes in our classes we group people by country of origin and tribe of origin. We have them debate and discuss the differences and similarities of their cultures. I have been involved in training in other venues that provided me with even wider exposure to individuals from other African countries.

This booklet has come out of all this experience. I have been teaching this for a long time and to many people from all over Africa. What has been the reaction of all these people to what I believe to be God's message to Africa? Well, as with the prophets of old, it has been varied and not always positive.

It is interesting to note that all of the groups, regardless of where they come from in Africa, agree 100% on the description of the Africa worldview. They may have different names for some of the concepts or spiritual beings discussed, but the meanings are consistent throughout Africa.

Reactions:

Many say that they have never been fully aware of their cultural framework. They have not understood why their people think, judge, react, and have the values they have. The teaching of God's message to Africa began to clarify this for them. The majority has wanted much more teaching on how to transform the African mind, starting with their own minds.

This also began to raise serious questions as to why the traditional teaching of the church as brought by the missionaries in the past and cemented by the present church leaders has not addressed this. This is much more than a blind spot that was ignored by church hierarchy. It could be excused, perhaps, of the missionaries from other continents who are unaware of African culture. However, it has become an issue of intimidation from the existing church structure, which does not want to see change. Pastors and church leaders who want to progress in the church structure, or who want a posting to a church with prominence, or even get paid the meager salary that might be available, soon find out that they must not shake the boat. This is true, not only in the United Methodist church, but in most denominations.

This has been the reaction of the students we have had, and the reaction of the leaders of the United Methodist Church in Congo. But some have said, "Oh, those pastors at Kafakumba Pastors' School have a low education and can't be representative of the type of leaders the church needs to promote." That is only partially true. Kafakumba Pastors' School trains the village pastors and many of them have only a high school education. However, I have taught in other venues and to quite a few different groups and denominations. Some of these have been at the continental level and some have been at the international level.

So I was curious as to what the reaction would be when I was asked to teach a workshop at Université Methodisté au Katanga (formerly Faculte Methodiste de Theologie Mulunguishi) to the graduating students who are the historical source of the Methodist church leaders. All of the Congolese Methodist bishops from all dioceses are the fruit of this institution of learning. In addition to the students, several of my former lecturers whom I have regarded as my "Gamaliels" attended the workshop I taught. Their reaction, as well as the students' reaction, was that for years they have been wondering about some of the behavior and attitude of the Christian community. The workshop opened their eyes.

This opportunity to speak also enabled me to go into further depth in some areas that were needing study. For instance:

- Reincarnation—what does it mean when a child is born with similar physical marks of the deceased on its body.
- Witchcraft—many examples were observed of this in charismatic groups who struggle with demon possession, fetishes, and other witchcraft practices.
- Dreams and visions

Obviously these are areas where satanic manipulation and deceit are playing havoc, psychological factors are involved, and genetics need to be explained.

Negative reactions:

The negative reactions I have observed have tended to be from individuals who came from areas where colonial abuse and power was strong. From areas where there was slavery, apartheid, and racism, which destroyed human dignity. These are people who see themselves as "Nehemiahs of Africa" who are going to rebuild their continent. Often they have been absent—whether for education or for other reasons. They are now back to "save" Africa. They have invested their time, money, energy, and lives in the work of building up African dignity and self worth. Consequently, when I have the audacity to question African culture, they see it as throwing in doubt all they are committed to. The reason usually given for their rejection is that it is scientifically unsound because there has been no research done.

My response to these "Nehemiahs" is that I respect and admire their dreams and sacrifices. I can see that Africa looks like Jerusalem at the time of Nehemiah. There is a need for people of ambition and courage like Nehemiah. But we need to be realistic. There are facts we have to consider very carefully.

- Nehemiah's motivation was not bitterness and hatred, as is often the case with these modern-day "Nehemiah's", but was the Lord's call.
- The modern-day "Nehemiah's" have not researched African culture to understand what they are espousing.
- The Old Testament Nehemiah's approach was based on God's revelation.
- After Jerusalem's wall was rebuilt, Nehemiah's job was only half done. It also involved reforming the people, and Nehemiah's tool, starting in Chapter 8, for that task was the Word of God.

- He used:
  - Mass mobilization of his people
  - Mass information of God's revelation
  - Mass motivation and support for the work
- The restoration involved:
  - Physical rebuilding of walls and buildings
  - Restoration of respect and fear of God
  - Social reforms
  - Restoration of peace, human dignity, and prosperity

This example of Nehemiah should be a model for our approach in dealing with the program of rebuilding Africa. Blind protectionism, bitterness and false self-esteem will never make the difference needed. It will without a doubt make things worse.

Mobutu tried the strategy of unquestioning promotion of Africanism. He used as a slogan, "Nous voulons être nous-mêmes, et non ce que les autres voudraient que nous soyons." It basically meant, "We want to be what we want to be and not what others want us to be." He promoted rejection of anything Western, including names and dress. He thought if traditional customs were restored, it would restore his country. However, the opposite effect has happened. We are worse than a joke. We are a shame and a disaster. Congolese are now among the most unwanted people in the world. African names and African dress are surface matters. The foundation he was building on was not sound, and nothing could stand.

My fellow Africans, you who are afraid of my approach, I love Africa. I know Africa. I ask you to not be afraid to question something, which comes from man. Our culture was formed by men and needs transformation. It needs to become the Africa God intended it to be.

CHAPTER 11 - WHAT GOD REQUIRES TO BRING TRANSFORMATION TO A NATION

The power of God to transform a society remains one of the most debatable topics on which people speculate, especially when facing natural and social tragedies. For instance, when observing the picture below, the most curious evidence that hits the eye of people who have attended my seminars is the fact that most of the countries in Africa which are being increasingly affected by social man-made tragedies, such as HIV-AIDS and ethnic wars, are unfortunately among the most Christianized countries in the world. Just refer to the picture below and judge for yourself.

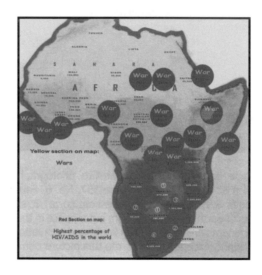

Upon observing this picture, many of the seminar participants question the transforming power of God with regard to social issues. And questions like the following are raised.

- Does God really have the power to bring transformation to nations like D. R. Congo, Liberia, Ruanda, Cote d' Ivoire, Burundi, etc.?
- If the answer is yes, why are these countries still becoming worse? Is there something lacking that prevents God from acting?

Some participants, acting as God's lawyers, try to justify this situation by saying that God's transforming power cannot deal with the social or material issues of a nation. God's transforming power deals with spiritual and moral matters of an individual because the time of total transformation has not come yet.

In this chapter, I want to invite you, my fellow African Christians, first to listen carefully to what God Himself says about these crucial problems, and then secondly to have the courage to look into yourself and see what it is that is lacking in our African Christianity.

God's Answer

First of all, God starts by revealing His will for His people. This is what the Lord says, *"For I know the thoughts that I think toward you, says the Lord, thoughts of peace and not of evil, to give you a future and a hope."* (Jeremiah 29: 1 NKJV)

You may feel you are going through impossible situations, but the Bible says, *"Now to him who is able to do immeasurably more than all we ask or imagine, according to his power that is at work within us."* (Ephesians 3:20 NIV)

Secondly, God reveals what really prevents Him from fulfilling the wonderful plans He has for His people. The prophet Isaiah says, *"Behold the Lord's hand is not shortened, that it cannot save; nor His ear heavy, that it cannot hear. But your iniquities have separated you from your God; And your sins have hidden His face from you, so that He will not hear."* (Isaiah 59:1-2 NKJV)

To clarify this, let me explain it through a practical example. We all know that a child is the fruit of a combined action of two different beings, a male and a female. Without each one there is no way to have a child. So both male and female are essential. It could be said that there is a parallel in the process of transformation of a nation. It is in fact a combined action between two different entities, one divine and another human. One is God, the other is His people. God wants His people to be involved in the process of total transformation of a nation or society. In God's eyes, His people are His irrigation pipes on earth, His field. Through them He wants to reach every dry society with His living and refreshing water. For that reason there are four fundamental requirements His people must fulfill.

This is what the Lord declares,

"If my people, which are called by my name, shall humble themselves and pray and seek my face and turn from their wicked ways, then will I hear from heaven and will forgive their sins and will heal their land." (II Chronicles 7:14 KJV)

I beg you, my brothers and sisters in Christ, to pay full attention to what our Lord means in these Scriptures.

He states that He has "good plans" for us, His people. He wants to give us "hope and a good future" and heal our land. But He clearly points out four requirements: humility, prayer, obedience and repentance or turning from our wicked ways. Please notice here that these four requirements are comparable to four batteries in a radio. For the radio to play, all four batteries are needed; otherwise nothing will happen. That is exactly the same with our Lord. Let us look attentively at these requirements (batteries).

1. HUMILITY

"If my people . . . shall humble themselves. . . "

To humble oneself has been differently interpreted by different people. But here it simply means the recognition of your real social status in the Kingdom of God, and the purpose for which you are here on earth; then acting and behaving accordingly.

When God requires His people to humble themselves, it is because all through the history of creation, His people have forgotten that they were on earth simply as His people-in-mission, for God's service and God's glory. Instead they rejected God's lordship and authority. They made themselves the masters on earth. Since then, for God to involve Himself in their business, He first requires them to recognize both their servanthood (status) and God's lordship, leadership and ownership in everything on earth and in heaven—land, sea, people (power), all creatures. . .

Now let us look back at our situation in Africa. Obviously Africa is actually known as the most fertile continent in the world for the work of evangelism. Millions and millions of people in Africa claim themselves to be God's men and God's women. This is very remarkable. In the countries like D. R. Congo, Zambia, Ruanda, Uganda bars and garages are being turned into worship points. In fact, there are plenty of people for God to use to bring transformation and prosperity in an amazing way. But unfortunately God still keeps quite. Why is God so silent? Does He not see all these atrocities being perpetrated on these very countries?

Before looking at the answer, I suggest we first take a look at ourselves, God's people, to see if we really deserve God's involvement in our struggles.

An interesting event has just taken place in one of the largest and most charismatic denominations in D. R. Congo. The aging top leader was in his last days on earth. There was obviously a need to select a successor before he died. So a group of respectable church leaders come to see him about this matter. Very relaxed, with a large smile, the old man simply said to them, "People of God, you are needlessly worried. That issue has already been solved. Do you not know that God Himself set us an example? Whom did He appoint as the King of His Kingdom if not His own Son, Jesus Christ? Was there any need for election? So also in my case, I have already chosen my successor. It is going to be my "beloved son". Please go back and forget about elections."

This event is just a reflection of what is going on in most of the churches in Africa. The issue of electing leaders in the church is far worse than electing political leaders. In an endeavor to consolidate their power and position in the church, claiming to be "God's people" they have come to a point where they are using any and all means, even wicked ones, in order to win the elections. These means include corruption, fetishes, dictatorships, intimidation, persecution, false accusation, assassination, etc. These all have become current strategic means in Christian organizations. Some denominations have become simply ethnic kingdoms where members from other tribes are treated as enemies or second class members. Consequently this has led many to create their own churches, causing the proliferation of innumerable independent sects and ministries.

Can we then say that in this kind of organization God owns leadership? Do you see there, any sign of humility? Is there any effort to show respect, honor, and glory to the Lord? I am without any doubt that God is not going to let Himself be involved in such shameful confusion. I am sure that the Lord is not going to act as long as this people, His people, keep making themselves kings and masters on earth without any consideration for God's lordship and their own status as servants.

2. PRAYER

". . . and pray . . ."

The interpretation of prayer in this passage is often misunderstood. The meaning of prayer in this context should not be separated from the first requirement, to humble oneself. Prayer here should be considered as one of the public acts of humility. For humility without public acts is meaningless and worthless. After the recognition of both their servanthood status and God's Lordship, the immediate act and attitude is simply to bow down at the feet of the one to whom you have denied respect and honor, and glorify His ownership and lordship.

Bowing down is one way of expressing to the Master and to the world that:
• I have totally surrendered myself to you, my Lord; I will no longer live for myself but for your honor and glory.

40

- I beg your grace and forgiveness for being in rebellion against you, my Lord.
- I now completely submit myself to your service and glory. From now on it will be no more my will, but Thy will done on earth as it is in heaven.

That is the right attitude of the second requirement. Expressing humility through open and public acts of our confession. We are asked to show to the world that all people, power, leadership, assignment, honor, glory, the church, ministries . . . belong only to our Lord.

3. SEEKING GOD'S FACE

"and seek my face . . ."

Like prayer, seeking God's face should also be understood as a second immediate act of humility. A Luba proverb says, "Mambo ne mukulu; wimuka—wimuka watala kwādi." The meaning is that when you are in court, if you are lucky enough to have the presiding judge to be an elder person of yours (i.e. a relative), make sure that you first look at him before you say or do anything. We look someone in the face to read his/her heart.

The face shows emotions more clearly than anything else. As servants of God, we need to make sure that the Lord and owner of all creation is not left out of our daily activities, dreams, emotions, etc. We should first seek His face; meaning His will, His guidance, His directives, His wisdom and His approval. For as a creator, the Lord owns everything, and everything on earth and in heaven is for His glory and honor. So it appears to be a grave offense to God when we manage our personal lives, our family, our church, our business, or our nation without any regard to God's face.

How often do we seek God's face when selecting and assigning people in God's field? How often do we seek God's face when making crucial decisions in our life, our business, our family or our society?

Seeking God's face is not only about worship, prayer and offerings. It is mostly about obeying God's spiritual, moral and social principles. That is why, in the book of Matthew 28: 19 – 20, Jesus assigns us a great commission. "*Go therefore and make disciples of all the nations, baptizing them in the name of the Father and of the Son and of the Holy Spirit, "teaching them to observe (OBEY) all things that I have commanded you;* (and then follows His great promise to us.) *And lo, I am with you always*, (I will be with you always, not just for a short while, but*) even to the end of the age."* (NKJV) Knowing that it is not safe for any man or woman of God to be alone in this corrupt and congested society, we are assured of His permanent presence and companionship so that whatever we face, He is there to lead and direct us.

Let me point out also that at times, God may ask us to do things that seem to us nonsense or bizarre. It does not matter; just obey and do it. Leave the result to Him. The attitude of Mary, Simon Peter and others should be a good example for us. When God asked Mary, a virgin, to have a child through the Holy Spirit, Mary just said, "I am the Lord's servant. May your word to me be fulfilled." (Luke 1:38 NIV) And Peter, after fishing all night without any catch, the Lord asked him to let down the nets for a daytime catch. He also just said, *"Master, we've worked hard all night and haven't caught anything. But because you say so, I will let down the nets."* (Luke 5: 4-5 NIV) For the Bible says, *"Does the LORD delight in burnt offerings and sacrifices as much as in obeying the LORD? To obey is better than sacrifice, and to heed is better than the fat of rams."* (I Samuel 15:22 NIV) And as one man of God said one day, "God treasures simple acts of obedience more than our prayers, praise or offerings."

4. TURN FROM THEIR WICKED WAYS

". . . and turn from their wicked ways . . ."

This is the third act of humility. The apostles Peter and Paul who seem to have better understanding than anyone else of this fundamental requirement explain it in this way.

"As obedient children of God, do not conform to the evil desires you had when you lived in ignorance. But just as He who called you is holy, so be holy in all you do; for it is written, 'Be holy, because I am holy.'" (I Peter 1:14 NIV)

"So from now on we regard no one from a worldly point of view. Though we once regarded Christ in this way, we do so no longer. Therefore, if anyone is in Christ, he is a new creation; the old has gone, the new has come! . . . we are therefore Christ's ambassadors." (II Corinthians 5: 16, 17, 20 NIV)

In other words, since the Lord our God is a God who never changes, we His people should also be like Him, a people who do not behave like chameleons, which for self-centered motives and ambitions, change constantly the color of their skin according to the environment they are in.

The Lord Jesus Christ says it in a very simple but very significant way, *"All you need to say is simply 'Yes' or 'No'; anything beyond this comes from the evil one."* (Matthew 5:37 NIV)

So, through this requirement, the people of God are asked to *"Give back to Caesar what is Caesar's and to God what is God's."* (Mark 12:17; Luke 20:22. NIV) Therefore, God wants his people to get completely rid of any wicked belief or act of our former sinful nature, namely *"sexual immorality, impurity and debauchery; idolatry and witchcraft, hatred, discord, jealousy, fits of rage, selfish ambition, dissension, factions and envy, drunkenness, orgies, and the like."* (Galatians 5:19-21 NIV)

It is obvious that this last requirement is the most costly and the most difficult to fulfill. In fact, a lot of men and women of God for their self-centered motives and ambitions, fail to *"distinguish between the holy and the common, . . . the clean and the unclean."* (Ezekiel 22:26-28. NIV)

This is the most difficult to fulfill because it deeply affects our personal dreams and ambitions, our relationship with our family, our friends, our social and church authorities, our business, and our moral and social ways of thinking and acting. For this reason, we shut our eyes and mouths about current issues that are blowing and eroding the foundations of our moral and social values. The pendulum of interpretation has swung to say that repentance is sorrow for sin. We feel that if we are sorry, we have repented. We no longer believe that changing our behavior or lifestyle needs to be involved. That is not the kind of people God can use to bring transformation to a nation. The Lord our God wants a people who are able to stand and say "no"; not a people who are ashamed to proclaim the principles of the Kingdom of God.

If we don't admit we are wrong, we can never correct anything. If we continue to blame others for our problems, we will continue as we are, and the "solutions" offered by the ones who we "blame" will continue to be as disastrous as they have been so far. We must admit our pride and our sinfulness. Only then will God be able to administer His "Theotherapy."

This "Theotherapy" (see page 45) will go after the cancer in our societies. It will not be fun or feel good. But we must continue to be honest before God and allow Him to purify us. We must not make excuses for ourselves. We must open every aspect of our culture, worldviews and societies to His "Theotherapy" and then trust that He will "heal our land" as He promised.

CHAPTER 12 - HOW GOD ACTS TO BRING TRANSFORMATION TO A NATION

Once the people of God begin to act and behave in total obedience to the Lord, then God starts the process of transformation. According to the scriptures, this process consists mainly in three acts of: hearing, forgiving and healing.

1. GOD HEARS HIS PEOPLE

"Then will I hear from heaven . . ."

God's first act for transformation is to hear His people. One could wonder why in Isaiah 59: 1-2, God could not hear the prayers and cries of his people; but now here He has accepted to hear His people? The reason is very simple. Here is God's answer, *"Because your heart was responsive and you humbled yourself before God when you heard what he spoke against this place and its people, and because you humbled yourself before me and tore your robes and wept in my presence, I have heard you."* (II Chronicles 34:27 NIV)

He does so because He is the God who hears the cries of humility and repentance. As someone wrote, "Where there is much repentance, there will be abundant grace." *"For whoever exalts himself will be humbled, and whoever humbles himself will be exalted."* (Matthew 23:12 NIV)

This act of hearing shows that God has accepted your repentance. *"For he who avenges blood remembers; he does not ignore the cry of the afflicted."* (Psalm 9:12 NIV) *"If you return to the Almighty, you will be restored; if you remove wickedness far from your tent and assign your nuggets to the dust, your gold of Ophir to the rocks in the ravines, then the Almighty will be your gold, the choicest silver for you. Surely then you will find delight in the Almighty and will lift up your face to God."* (Job 22:23-26 NIV)

2. GOD FORGIVES

". . . and I will forgive their sins . . ."

The second act of God in the process of transformation is forgiveness. The Bible declares, *"If we confess our sins he is faithful and just and will forgive us our sins and purify us from all unrighteousness."* (I John 1:9 NIV) for *"the Lord our God is merciful and forgiving, even though we have rebelled against him."* (Daniel 9:9 NIV)

And when our Lord forgives, it means He washes our sins away and forgets forever. The Bible says, *"though your sins are like scarlet, they shall be as white as snow; though they are red as crimson, they shall be like wool."* (Isaiah 1:18 NIV)

3. GOD HEALS

". . . and will heal their land."

Some of the contemporary Bible translators are not comfortable with the word "heal" in this verse. Instead they substitute it with words like prosper, restore . . . But I do believe the God is fully aware of the meaning of every word He uses. When He says He will "heal" their land, the word "heal" should be understood as such. The reason is that a country may be economically and technologically prosperous, but still have very serious infections and diseases of all kinds: physical, moral, social and spiritual. The U.S.A. and the Republic of South Africa obviously have this disposition.

So substituting "to heal" with other words limits the deepness of the healing act of God. The Bible says, *"Praise the Lord, O my soul, and forget not all his benefits—who forgives all your sins and heals all your diseases, who redeems your life from the pit and crowns you with love and compassion, who satisfies your desires with good things so that your youth is renewed like the eagle."* (Psalm 103: 2-5 NIV)

God's act of healing the country has to do with much more than the simple material prosperity. It deals with every kind of injury and disease that affects a country. (II Kings 2:21 – 22; Jeremiah 30:17) For *"with man this is impossible, but with God all things are possible."* (Matthew 19:26 NIV)

Beloved fellow Africans, the ball is in our court. The problem is not the tree (Africa). It is the ground (African worldview) and the shameful lack of humility of God's people. The Lord our God is ready to hear our cries and involve Himself in our struggles. But He cannot do it as long as there is yet no sign of humility among His own people.

Remember the story of Sodom. Sodom's sin was far deeper than ours. But God was still ready to forgive and heal the entire city if there could be at least TEN humbled men and women! (Genesis 18: 16-33)

So there is also hope for Africa—and for all nations. It is just a matter humbling ourselves. The Lord says,

"Now return to me, and I will return to you. I will sprinkle clean water on you, and you will be clean; I will cleanse you from all your impurities and from your idols. I will give you a new heart and put a new spirit in you; I will remove from you your heart of stone and give you a heart of flesh. And I will put my Spirit in you and move you to follow my decrees and be careful to keep my laws . . . I am the Lord and I do not change." (Ezekiel 36:25 – 27 NIV)

BIBLIOGRAPHY

Picture NASA Earth City Lights 1994; Credit: Image by Craig Mayhew and Robert Simmon, NASA GSFC.

TWEETEN, LON Graphic Artist; "Death Stalks a Continent," *Time*, Vol. 157, No 6, February 12, 2001, pp. 46 – 55.

Webster/s New World College Dictionary, 1999, Page 1650

ABOUT THE AUTHOR

Kasongo Munza was an ordained pastor in the United Methodist Church, North Katanga Conference in D.R. Congo. He had been in the Lord's service since 1977. First as a pastor in rural areas; then as a District Superintendent, Evangelist, Director of Christian Education, General Secretary of the Central Conference of D.R. Congo, and Bishop's Assistant. He was serving the church as the Director of Kafakumba Training Center in Zambia, Africa, when he was diagnosed with Non-Hodgkin's Lymphoma. He passed away in October 2005

He was married to Ilunga and had six children.

Printed in the United States
By Bookmasters